PIANO · VOCAL · GUITAR

CMT 100 Greatest SONGS of country music

W9-BBX-402

Cover photo © Nubar Alexanian/Corbis

ISBN 0-634-06352-9

HAL•LEONARD® CORPORATION

7777 W. BLUEMOUND RD. P.O. BOX 13819 MILWAUKEE, WI 53213

Visit Hal Leonard Online at
www.halleonard.com

INTRODUCTION

Country music has very effectively defined and established itself as America's soundtrack. It's become the home of this country's story in song. Throughout its history, country music has been very much peer group music—songwriters writing about the immediate concerns of everybody in the community, people telling stories about their lives to their friends and neighbors and the greater community.

Songwriting in country music began to be centered in Nashville with the establishment of Acuff-Rose Publications, the first major American song publishing house outside New York or Los Angeles. This venerable music publishing firm—home to some of the most distinguished song copyrights in music, from works by artists ranging from Hank Williams to Roy Orbison to the Everly Brothers—is perhaps the main reason that Nashville became the home of country music. Had it not been for Acuff-Rose, Atlanta or Cincinnati or Chicago or any of several other cities might well have developed into the center of country music.

Acuff-Rose was formed in 1942, in an era when Nashville was just one of many cities with a country barn dance broadcast on the radio—the Grand Ole Opry on WSM—that competed with such powerhouses as station WLS and its National Barn Dance in Chicago, Cincinnati's Barn Dance on WLW, Boston's Hayloft Jamboree on WCOP, the Hayloft Hoedown on WFIL in Philadelphia, KRLD's Big D Jamboree in Dallas, and Shreveport's Louisiana Hayride on KWKH. Los Angeles had the Hollywood Barn Dance on KNX and the Hometown Jamboree on KXLA. Atlanta's WSB was the first radio station in the South and became a country giant. Atlanta was also the site of many early country field recordings by the New York record labels. Most pre-World War II country recording was done in New York City, where WHN's Barn Dance competed with other New York country stations. New York was also the world's music publishing capital.

Acuff-Rose was the first music publisher in Nashville. It was a curious partnership. Roy Acuff was a staunch hillbilly singer—as country singers were known then—from East Tennessee, who was so famous that when Japanese troops attacked American forces in the Pacific during World War II, their battle cry was often "To hell with [President Franklin] Roosevelt, to hell with Babe Ruth, to hell with Roy Acuff." (Interestingly, the "Acuff" in "Acuff-Rose" actually stood for Mildred Acuff, Roy's wife, who was the de facto partner in the partnership.) Acuff's partner Fred Rose was a recovering alcoholic, a Christian Scientist and an accomplished Tin Pan Alley songwriter out of Chicago. He had written pop hits for Gene Autry and Sophie Tucker, and penned such songs as "Blue Eyes Crying in the Rain," which many years later became Willie Nelson's first No. 1 single.

When Fred Rose discovered a raw, young Alabama writer and singer named Hank Williams in 1946, he found Nashville's future, as well as his own. Rose groomed Williams like a son and so thoroughly coached him and polished his songs that to this day experts cannot agree on just how much of Williams' songwriting genius was actually due to the old pro's work.

Nashville became firmly implanted on the music map by the crossover success of Williams' songs. Rose was able to call on his friend Mitch Miller, the head of A&R at Columbia Records in New York, to place Williams' songs with pop artists. As the likes of Tony Bennett, Rosemary Clooney, and Jo Stafford had success with Williams' songs, the crossover appeal of Nashville songs became very apparent. Patti Page had a No. 1 pop hit with the Acuff-Rose song "Tennessee Waltz."

Record labels began to set up permanent offices in Nashville. RCA, Decca, and Columbia established beachheads in Nashville and recording studios sprang up. More song publishers began to be attracted to Nashville. The Music City identity began to evolve.

Following the record labels and song publishers, songwriters began to be drawn to Nashville. Great songwriters such as Harlan Howard, Dolly Parton, Fred Rose, Cindy Walker, Willie Nelson, Gretchen Peters, Don Gibson, Leslie Satcher, Johnny Cash, Kris Kristofferson, Bobby Braddock, Loretta Lynn, Roger Miller, Don Schlitz, Dwight Yoakam, Mickey Newbury, Tom T. Hall, and many others made Nashville their home as they told captivating tales about the human condition. Their three-minute sagas capture the true grit and drama of everyday life.

There are songs of unrequited love, lost love, lost love avenged, dead babies, killing, lust, anger, funerals, heaven, hell, money, crime, children, wives, husbands, daughters, sons, mothers, fathers, grandparents, farms, cities, cowboys, patriotism, cowgirls, rodeos, prison, trains, trucks, revenge, cars, car races, car wrecks, guns, airplanes, boats, food, ships, dogs, horses, horse races, best friends, gamblers, beer, whiskey, tequila, wine, winos, Elvis, Jesus, Satan, coal mines, rescues from coal mines, death in coal mines, killers, the Bible, war, the American flag, peace, work, fishing, and hunting.

Sometimes the song titles capture you immediately with their human immediacy: "Born to Lose," "Pick Me Up on Your Way Down," "Don't Let Me Cross Over," "If I Could Hear My Mother Pray Again," "Friends in Low Places," "I'm Just an Old Chunk of Coal (But I'm Gonna Be a Diamond Someday)," "That's the Way Love Goes," "Funny How Time Slips Away," "She Thinks I Still Care," "Take These Chains from My Heart," "I'm So Lonesome I Could Cry," "It Makes No Difference Now," "They'll Never Take Her Love from Me," "How Do You Like Me Now!?," "On the Other Hand," "Don't Come Home a Drinkin' (With Lovin' on Your Mind)," "It Wasn't God Who Made Honky Tonk Angels," "Stand by Your Man," "There Stands the Glass," "Is There Life Out There," "He Thinks He'll Keep Her," and "Walkaway Joe." Just from the titles, you know what they're talking about and you sense what you're about to hear.

Billy Joe Shaver's hardscrabble "Honky Tonk Heroes" jostles comfortably against Fred Rose's elegant "Blue Eyes Crying in the Rain" and Gretchen Peters' anthemic modern-day "Independence Day." You can smell the honky tonk's pungent sawdust on the floor, feel the insistent throb of the jukebox, and taste the sharp whiskey in Webb Pierce's evocative "There Stands the Glass."

Kinky Friedman's emotionally charged song about the Holocaust, "Ride 'em Jewboy," defines country music as succinctly as does Roy Acuff's epochal tale of personal mayhem brought on by the advent of the automobile, "Wreck on the Highway," or the Carter Family's mystical "Wildwood Flower."

Saga songs such as "North to Alaska," "The Battle of New Orleans," and "Amelia Earhart's Last Flight" chronicle important events in American history. Hank Williams directed his "No, No Joe" at Russian dictator Joseph Stalin.

Big, rollicking songs full of gusto such as "Roly Poly"—the great Fred Rose as song-writer again—as sung by Bob Wills and His Texas Playboys, and Hank Thompson's "A Six Pack to Go" capture America's fun-loving spirit. That spirit has been echoed in such songs as Little Jimmy Dickens' "May the Bird of Paradise Fly up Your Nose" and Brad Paisley's "I'm Gonna Miss Her (The Fishin' Song)." Writer Steve Goodman and artist David Allan Coe captured "the perfect country song" in "You Never Even Called Me by My Name" because, as Coe explains during the song, it includes the basic country music elements of prison, trains, trucks, Mamma, and getting drunk.

Loretta Lynn pre-dated much of the feminist agenda with such bold personal statements as "Fist City," "The Pill," and "Don't Come Home a Drinkin' (With Lovin' on Your Mind)." The great "Waiting for a Train," by the "Father of Country Music," Jimmie Rodgers, still conjures up the lure of the open road and the mystique of the train. It is beautifully complemented by the Dixie Chicks' similarly-themed "Wide Open Spaces."

Tony Arata's "The Dance," as recorded by Garth Brooks, is a delicate, elegant, and timeless comment on the human condition.

War, national tragedy and patriotism have long been staples of country music, from "There's a Star-Spangled Banner Waving Somewhere" to "The Ballad of the Green Berets" to "Where Have All Our Heroes Gone." Alan Jackson's heartfelt "Where Were You (When the World Stopped Turning)" beautifully depicted the personal human significance of 9/11 and was bookended by Toby Keith's angry "Courtesy of the Red, White and Blue (The Angry American)" and Charlie Daniels' equally defiant "This Ain't No Rag, It's a Flag." Lee Greenwood's "God Bless the U.S.A." continues as a patriotic standard.

Leon Payne's chilling song "Psycho" (which has attracted cover versions as spot-on as Elvis Costello's) tells the narrator's icy tale of serial killing. Porter Wagoner's twisted "Rubber Room" takes the listener to places perhaps unwanted and feared. When Wagoner sings "When a man sees things and hears sounds that's not there / He's headed for the rubber room," you sense that this is not a traditional country song.

The pop side of country has been evocatively captured in song by artists ranging from Faith Hill to Eddy Arnold, from Shania Twain to Ray Price, from John Denver to Olivia Newton-John, and from Charlie Rich to Patsy Cline.

Defining country music's one hundred greatest songs may seem to be a bit of a conceit. It's certainly a daunting task. Of the thousands and thousands of country songs, what songs could possibly be the "100 Greatest"? It's a great parlor game, and one that we discovered is the basis for endless office discussions, barroom rants, late night phone calls and e-mails. Favorite country songs are very personal to listeners. Letters, phone calls, and e-mails to country artists are full of personal testimony to what those songs mean in listener's lives. These songs mean the world to them. "Hank Williams, You Wrote My Life" is as true today as it ever was.

—Chet Flippo

CHET FLIPPO

Chet Flippo is Editorial Director of CMT and CMT.com. Before joining CMT, he was Country Music Editor for Sonicnet.com. From 1995 until joining Sonicnet in 2000, he was *Billboard*'s Nashville Bureau Chief.

Flippo was born in Fort Worth, Texas, and served in the U.S. Navy during the Vietnam War and earned bachelor's and master's degrees in journalism. After working as Contributing Editor for *Rolling Stone* magazine while in graduate school at the University of Texas in Austin, he opened *Rolling Stone*'s New York bureau in 1974. After *Rolling Stone* moved its offices from San Francisco to New York in 1977, he became *Rolling Stone* Senior Editor. In addition to covering such artists and subjects as The Rolling Stones, Bob Dylan, John Lennon, Joseph Heller, Tom Wolfe, and The Who, he initiated country music coverage for *Rolling Stone*, profiling such artists as Willie Nelson, Dolly Parton, and Waylon Jennings.

He left *Rolling Stone* in 1980 to write the book *Your Cheatin' Heart: A Biography of Hank Williams* and since has written books on Paul McCartney, Graceland, The Rolling Stones, and David Bowie, and published an anthology of articles, *Everybody Was Kung-Fu Dancing*. He has also written articles for the *New York Times*, *TV Guide*, *Texas Monthly*, and *Q Magazine* of London, and other publications, and has written TV scripts for VH1 and CBS.

In the early 1990s, Flippo was a lecturer in journalism at the University of Tennessee in Knoxville, before moving to Nashville to work for *Billboard*. He received the Country Music Association's 1998 CMA Media Achievement Award.

RANK	SONG	ARTIST	YEAR
1.	Stand by Your Man	Tammy Wynette	1968
2.	He Stopped Loving Her Today	George Jones	1980
3.	Crazy	Patsy Cline	1961
4.	Ring of Fire	Johnny Cash	1963
5.	Your Cheatin' Heart	Hank Williams	1953
6.	Friends in Low Places	Garth Brooks	1990
7.	I Fall to Pieces	Patsy Cline	1961
8.	Galveston	Glen Campbell	1969
9.	Behind Closed Doors	Charlie Rich	1973
10.	Mammas Don't Let Your Babies Grow Up to Be Cowboys	Waylon Jennings & Willie Nelson	1978
11.	Blue Moon of Kentucky	Bill Monroe	1954
12.	Amarillo by Morning	George Strait	1983
13.	Coal Miner's Daughter	Loretta Lynn	1970
14.	The Dance	Garth Brooks	1990
15.	Forever and Ever, Amen	Randy Travis	1987
16.	I Will Always Love You	Dolly Parton	1974, 1982
17.	Hello Darlin'	Conway Twitty	1970
18.	Take Me Home, Country Roads	John Denver	1971
19.	Hey, Good Lookin'	Hank Williams	1951
20.	I Am a Man of Constant Sorrow	Soggy Bottom Boys	2000
21.	Okie from Muskogee	Merle Haggard	1968
22.	Wide Open Spaces	Dixie Chicks	1999
23.	Blue Eyes Crying in the Rain	Willie Nelson	1975
24.	The Chair	George Strait	1985
25.	Folsom Prison Blues	Johnny Cash	1955, 1968
26.	The Gambler	Kenny Rogers	1978
27.	Fancy	Reba McEntire	1991
28.	Where Were You (When the World Stopped Turning)	Alan Jackson	2001
29.	I'm So Lonesome I Could Cry	Hank Williams	1949
30.	I Hope You Dance	Lee Ann Womack	2000
31.	I Walk the Line	Johnny Cash	1956
32.	Rhinestone Cowboy	Glen Campbell	1975
33.	Always on My Mind	Willie Nelson	1982
34.	Harper Valley P.T.A.	Jeannie C. Riley	1968
35.	D-I-V-O-R-C-E	Tammy Wynette	1968
36.	Can the Circle Be Unbroken	The Carter Family	1935
		Nitty Gritty Dirt Band	1972
37.	King of the Road	Roger Miller	1965
38.	Breathe	Faith Hill	2000
39.	Make the World Go Away	Ray Price	1963
		Eddy Arnold	1965
40.	Hello Walls	Faron Young	1961
41.	Sweet Dreams	Patsy Cline	1963
42.	El Paso	Marty Robbins	1959
43.	Delta Dawn	Tanya Tucker	1972
44.	When I Call Your Name	Vince Gill	1990
45.	Guitars, Cadillacs	Dwight Yoakam	1986
46.	Desperado	Eagles	1972
47.	Don't Come Home a Drinkin' (With Lovin' on Your Mind)	Loretta Lynn	1966
48.	Boot Scootin' Boogie	Brooks & Dunn	1991
49.	I Can't Stop Loving You	Ray Charles	1972
		Don Gibson	1958
50.	Independence Day	Martina McBride	1994
51.	It Wasn't God Who Made Honky Tonk Angels	Kitty Wells	1952

RANK	SONG	ARTIST	YEAR
52.	On the Other Hand	Randy Travis	1986
53.	Walking the Floor Over You	Ernest Tubb	1941
54.	Coat of Many Colors	Dolly Parton	1971
55.	Act Naturally	Buck Owens	1963
56.	Mama He's Crazy	The Judds	1984
57.	If You've Got the Money (I've Got the Time)	Lefty Frizzell	1950
		Willie Nelson	1976
58.	Kiss an Angel Good Mornin'	Charley Pride	1971
59.	Family Tradition	Hank Williams, Jr.	1979
60.	Go Rest High on That Mountain	Vince Gill	1995
61.	Lovesick Blues	Hank Williams	1948
62.	Don't Rock the Jukebox	Alan Jackson	1991
63.	Tennessee Waltz	Patti Page	1951
64.	When You Say Nothing at All	Keith Whitley	1988
		Alison Krauss	1995
65.	God Bless the U.S.A.	Lee Greenwood	1985
66.	Green Green Grass of Home	Porter Wagoner	1965
67.	It's Your Love	Tim McGraw with Faith Hill	1997
68.	There Stands the Glass	Webb Pierce	1953
69.	The Devil Went Down to Georgia	Charlie Daniels	1979
70.	Chiseled in Stone	Vern Gosdin	1989
71.	Don't Toss Us Away	Patty Loveless	1988
72.	A Boy Named Sue	Johnny Cash	1969
73.	You Are My Sunshine	Jimmie Davis	1940
74.	Flowers on the Wall	The Statler Brothers	1965
75.	Strawberry Wine	Deana Carter	1996
76.	A Good Hearted Woman	Waylon Jennings & Willie Nelson	1976
77.	You're Still the One	Shania Twain	1998
78.	My Home's in Alabama	Alabama	1980
79.	Is There Life Out There	Reba McEntire	1991
80.	She's in Love with the Boy	Trisha Yearwood	1991
81.	Smoky Mountain Rain	Ronnie Milsap	1980
82.	Should've Been a Cowboy	Toby Keith	1993
83.	(I Never Promised You A) Rose Garden	Lynn Anderson	1970
84.	Please Remember Me	Tim McGraw	1999
85.	Blue	LeAnn Rimes	1996
86.	Before the Next Teardrop Falls	Freddy Fender	1975
87.	Passionate Kisses	Mary-Chapin Carpenter	1992
88.	Have I Told You Lately That I Love You	Gene Autry	1946
89.	Here's a Quarter (Call Someone Who Cares)	Travis Tritt	1991
90.	He'll Have to Go	Jim Reeves	1959
91.	Seven Year Ache	Rosanne Cash	1981
92.	Sunday Mornin' Comin' Down	Johnny Cash	1970
93.	Take This Job and Shove It	Johnny Paycheck	1978
94.	Something in Red	Lorrie Morgan	1991
95.	Foggy Mountain Breakdown	Flatt & Scruggs	1949
96.	I'd Be Better Off (In a Pine Box)	Doug Stone	1990
97.	Amazed	Lonestar	2000
98.	Faded Love	Bob Wills	1950
		Patsy Cline	1963
99.	Back in the Saddle Again	Gene Autry	1939
100.	Killin' Time	Clint Black	1989

ACT NATURALLY

Words and Music by VONIE MORRISON
and JOHNNY RUSSELL

ALWAYS ON MY MIND

Words and Music by WAYNE THOMPSON,
MARK JAMES and JOHNNY CHRISTOPHER

Amazed

Words and Music by MARV GREEN,
CHRIS LINDSEY and AIMEE MAYO

Moderately slow Country Ballad

Ev-'ry time our eyes meet, this feel-in' in-side me
The smell of your skin, the taste of your kiss,

is al-most more than I___ can take.___
the way you whis-per in___ the dark.___

*Recorded a half step lower.

AMARILLO BY MORNING

Words and Music by TERRY STAFFORD
and PAUL FRASIER

BACK IN THE SADDLE AGAIN

Words and Music by RAY WHITLEY
and GENE AUTRY

BEFORE THE NEXT TEARDROP FALLS

Words and Music by BEN PETERS
and VIVIAN KEITH

BEHIND CLOSED DOORS

Words and Music by
KENNY O'DELL

Verse

2. (My) baby makes me smile, Lord, don't she make me smile.
   She's never far away or too tired to say I want you.
   She's always a lady, just like a lady should be
   But when they turn out the lights, she's still a baby to me. **(Chorus)**

BLUE EYES CRYING IN THE RAIN

Words and Music by
FRED ROSE

BLUE

Words and Music by
BILL MACK

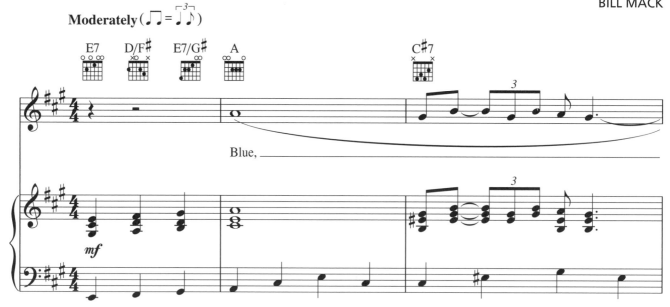

BLUE MOON OF KENTUCKY

Words and Music by
BILL MONROE

Bright jump tempo

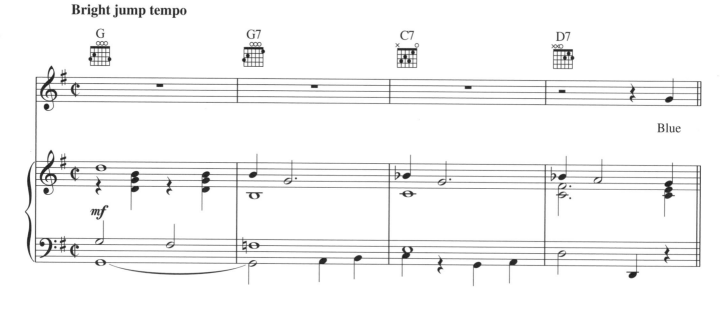

Blue

moon, _____ blue moon, _____ blue

moon _____ keep a - shin - in' bright. _____ Blue

BOOT SCOOTIN' BOOGIE

Words and Music by
RONNIE DUNN

A BOY NAMED SUE

Words and Music by
SHEL SILVERSTEIN

Moderately bright

(Spoken)
1. Well, my "daddy" left home when I was three, and he didn't leave much to ma and me. Just this old guitar and an empty bottle of booze. Now, I don't blame him because he run and hid, but the meanest thing that he ever did was be-

bust his head, I tell you, life ain't easy for A Boy Named Sue.

Well, Sue.

2. (Well,) I grew up quick and I grew up mean, My fist got hard and my wits got keen.
   Roamed from town to town to hide my shame, but I made me a vow to the moon and stars,
   I'd search the honky tonks and bars and kill that man that give me that awful name.

   But it was Gatlinburg in mid July and I had just hit town and my throat was dry.
   I'd thought I'd stop and have myself a brew. At an old saloon on a street of mud
   And at a table dealing stud sat the dirty, mangy dog that named me Sue.

3. Well I knew that snake was my own sweet dad from a worn-out picture that my mother had.
   And I know that scar on his cheek and his evil eye. He was big and bent and gray and old
   And I looked at him and my blood ran cold, and I said "My name is Sue. How do you do.

   Now you're gonna die. "Yeah, that's what I told him.

   Well I hit him right between the eyes and he went down, but to my surprise he come up with a knife
   And cut off a piece of my ear. But I busted a chair right across his teeth. And we crashed through
   The wall and into the street kicking and a-gouging in the mud and the blood and the beer.

4. I tell you I've fought tougher men but I really can't remember when.
   He kicked like a mule and he bit like a crocodile. I heard him laughin' and then I heard him cussin',
   He went for his gun and I pulled mine first. He stood there looking at me and I saw him smile,

   And he said, "Son, this world is rough and if a man's gonna make it, he's gotta be tough
   And I know I wouldn't be there to help you along. So I give you that name and I said 'Goodbye,'
   I knew you'd have to get tough or die. And it's that name that helped to make you strong.

5. Yeah, he said now you have just fought one helluva fight, and I know you hate me and you've
   Got the right to kill me now and I wouldn't blame you if you do. But you ought to thank me
   Before I die for the gravel in your guts and the spit in your eye because I'm the_ _ _ _
   That named you Sue."

   Yeah, what could I do? What could I do?

   I got all choked up and I threw down my gun. Called him a pa and he called me a son,
   And I come away with a different point of view. And I think about him now and then.
   Every time I tried, every time I win and if I ever have a son I think I am gonna name him
   Bill or George - - anything but Sue.

CAN THE CIRCLE BE UNBROKEN
(Will the Circle Be Unbroken)

Words and Music by
A.P. CARTER

BREATHE

Words and Music by HOLLY LAMAR
and STEPHANIE BENTLEY

Moderately fast

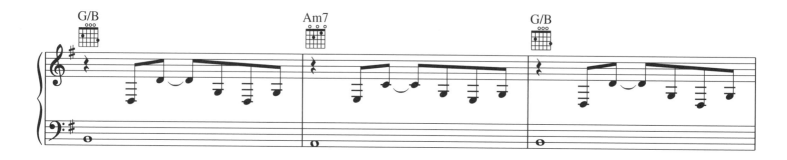
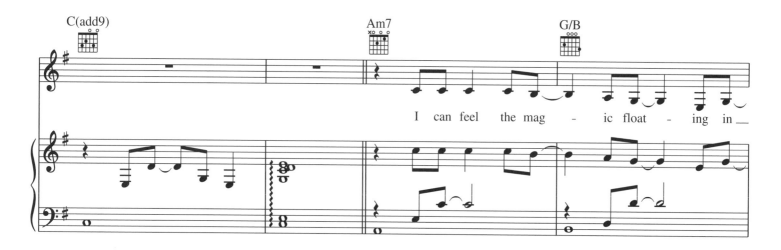
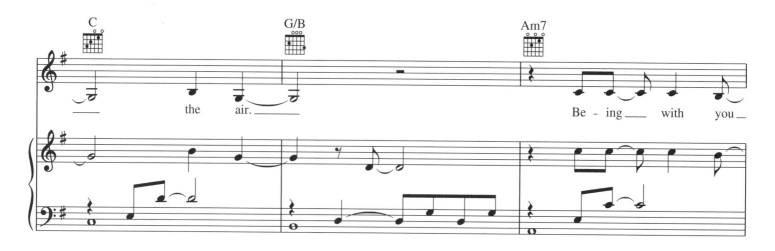

I can feel the mag - ic float - ing in

the air. Be - ing with you

58

THE CHAIR

Words and Music by HANK COCHRAN
and DEAN DILLON

Medium Slow

Well, ex- cuse __ me, __ but I think you've __ got my

chair.   No, that __ one's not tak - en; I __ don't

mind   if you __ sit here.   I'll be glad   to share. __ Yeah, it's u -

COAL MINER'S DAUGHTER

from COAL MINER'S DAUGHTER

Words and Music by
LORETTA LYNN

CHISELED IN STONE

Words and Music by MAX BARNES
and VERN GOSDIN

See addtional lyrics

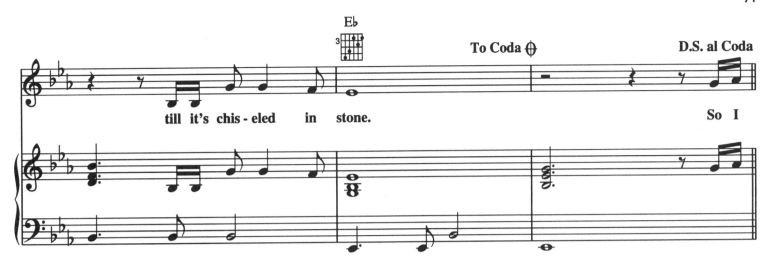

Additional Lyrics

2. Then an old man sat beside me
   And looked me in the eye.
   He said, "Son, I know what you're goin' through.
   But you oughta get down on your knees
   And thank your lucky stars
   That you've got someone to go home to."
   Chorus

3. So I brought these pretty flowers
   Hopin' you would understand
   Sometimes a man is such a fool.
   These golden words of wisdom
   From the heart of that old man
   Showed me I ain't nothin' without you.
   Chorus

COAT OF MANY COLORS

Words and Music by
DOLLY PARTON

Back through the years I go wan-d'ring once a-gain, back to the sea-sons of my youth. I re-call a box of rags that some-one gave us and

CRAZY

Words and Music by
WILLIE NELSON

D-I-V-O-R-C-E

Words and Music by BOBBY BRADDOCK
and CURLY PUTMAN

THE DANCE

Words and Music by
TONY ARATA

but I'd have had _ to _ miss _____ the _____

dance.

DELTA DAWN

Words and Music by ALEX HARVEY
and LARRY COLLINS

Del-ta ___ Dawn, what's that flow-er you have on? Could it be _

___ a fad-ed rose ___ from days gone by? And

did I hear you say ___ he was a-meet-in' you here to-day ___ to

DESPERADO

Words and Music by DON HENLEY
and GLENN FREY

THE DEVIL WENT DOWN TO GEORGIA

Words and Music by CHARLIE DANIELS, JOHN THOMAS CRAIN, JR.,
WILLIAM JOEL DiGREGORIO, FRED LAROY EDWARDS,
CHARLES FRED HAYWARD and JAMES WAINWRIGHT MARSHALL

Fast Hoedown

The

if you win, you get this shin - y fid - dle made of gold. But

if you lose, the dev - il gets your soul. _____

The dev - il o - pened up his case, and he

When the dev-il fin-ished, John-ny said, _ "Well, you're

Gran-ny, does your dog bite? No, child, no.

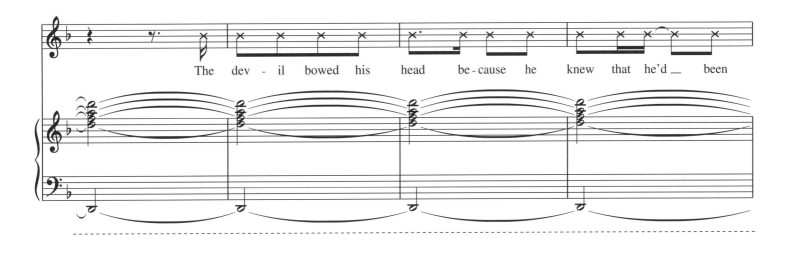

The dev-il bowed his head be-cause he knew that he'd _ been

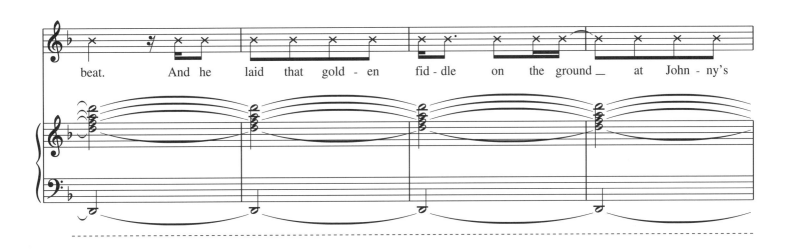

beat. And he laid that gold-en fid-dle on the ground _ at John-ny's

feet. John-ny said, "Dev-il, just come on back _ if you ev-er want to try a-gain. _

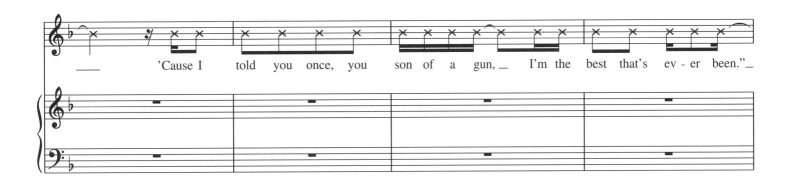

_ 'Cause I told you once, you son of a gun, _ I'm the best that's ev-er been." _

EL PASO

Words and Music by
MARTY ROBBINS

Moderato

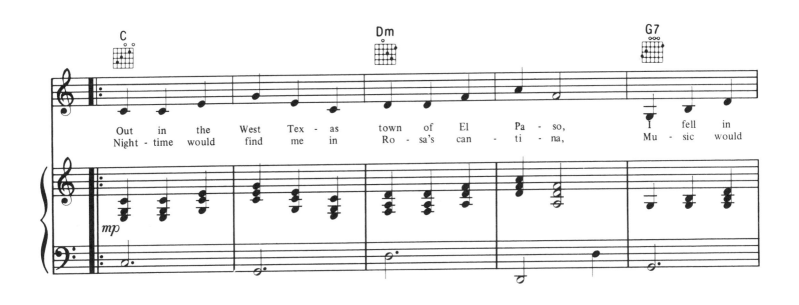

Out in the West Tex - as town of El Pa - so,　　I fell in
Night - time would West find me in Ro - sa's can - ti - na,　　Mu - sic would

love with a Mex - i - can girl.
play and Fe - li - na would

whirl.

112

DON'T COME HOME A DRINKIN'
(With Lovin' on Your Mind)

Words and Music by LORETTA LYNN
and PEGGY SUE WELLS

Well, you thought I'd be wait-in' up ___ when ___
nev - er take me an - y - where ___ be -

you came home last night.
cause you're al - ways gone.

You'd been out with all the boys ___ and you
And man - y a night ___ I've laid a - wake ___ and ___

DON'T ROCK THE JUKEBOX

Words and Music by ALAN JACKSON,
ROGER MURRAH and KEITH STEGALL

Additional Lyrics

2. I ain't got nothin' against rock and roll.
   But when your heart's been broken, you need a song that's slow.
   Ain't nothin' like a steel guitar to drown a memory.
   Before you spend your money, babe, play a song for me.
   Chorus

DON'T TOSS US AWAY

Words and Music by
BRYAN MACLEAN

D.S. al Coda

FADED LOVE

Words and Music by BOB WILLS
and JOHNNY WILLS

Moderato

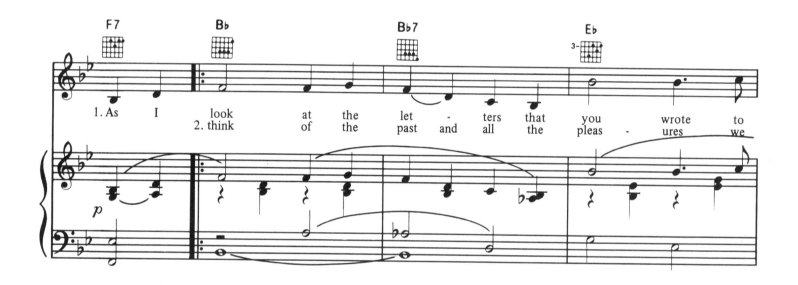

1. As I look at the let - ters that you wrote to
2. think of the past and all the pleas - ures we

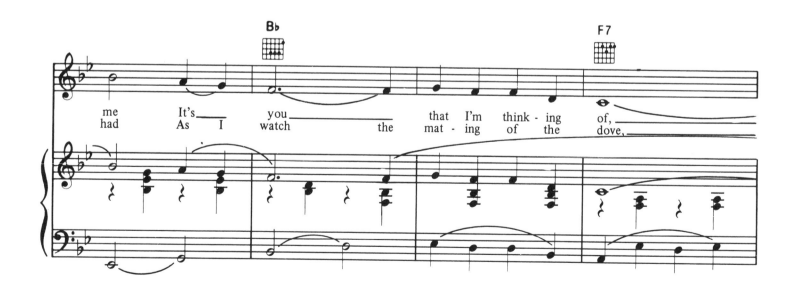

me had It's___ you_____ that I'm think - ing of,
As I watch the mat - ing of the dove,

FANCY

Words and Music by
BOBBIE GENTRY

let me down, ___ now, your ma-ma's gon - na move you up - town.

D.S. al Coda

CODA

Well,

It

was - n't long af - ter, a be - nev - o - lent man ___ took me in off the streets.

One week lat - er I was pour - in' his tea in a five - room ho - tel suite. I charmed a king, a

con - gress - man __ and an oc - ca - sion - al a - ris - to - crat. __ And then I got me a Geor - gia man -

F#5

- sion and an el - e - gant New York town - house flat and I ain't done bad.

A   B

F#5

Now, in this world there's a lot of self - right - eous

FAMILY TRADITION

Words and Music by
HANK WILLIAMS, JR.

1. Coun-try mu-sic sing-ers have al-ways been a real close fam-i-
2.,3. (See additional lyrics)

ly, But late-ly some of my kin-folk have dis-

owned a few oth-ers and me. ___ I guess it's be-

Additional Lyrics

2. I am very proud of my daddy's name,
Although his kind of music and mine ain't exactly the same
Stop and think it over, put yourself in my position
If I get stoned and sing all night long, it's a family tradition.

So don't ask me, "Hank,
Why do you drink?
Hank, why do you roll smoke?
Why must you live out the songs that you wrote?"
If I'm down in a honky tonk, some old slicks tryin' to give me friction
I say leave me alone, I'm singin' all night long, it's a family tradition.

3. Lordy, I have loved some ladies and I have loved Jim Beam
And they both tried to kill me in Nineteen Seventy Three
When that doctor asked me, "Son, how'd you get in this condition?"
I said, "Hey sawbones, I'm just carryin' on an old family tradition."

So don't ask me, "Hank,
Why do you drink?
Hank, why do you roll smoke?
Why must you live out the songs that you wrote?"
Stop and think it over, try to put yourself in my unique position
If I get stoned and sing all night long, it's a family tradition.

FLOWERS ON THE WALL

Words and Music by
LEWIS CALVIN DeWITT

Original key: G♯ minor. This edition has been transposed up one half-step to be more playable.

146

Smok - in' cig - a - rettes_ and watch - in' Cap - tain Kan - ga - roo,_

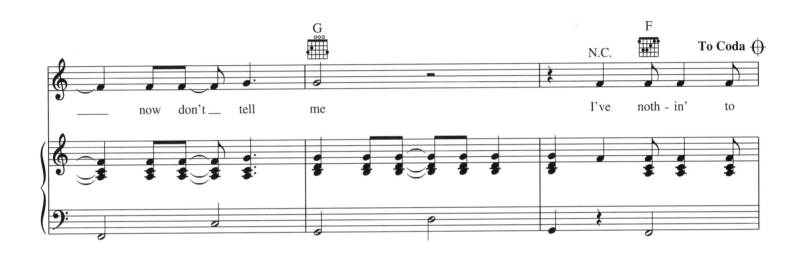

_____ now don't __ tell me I've noth - in' to

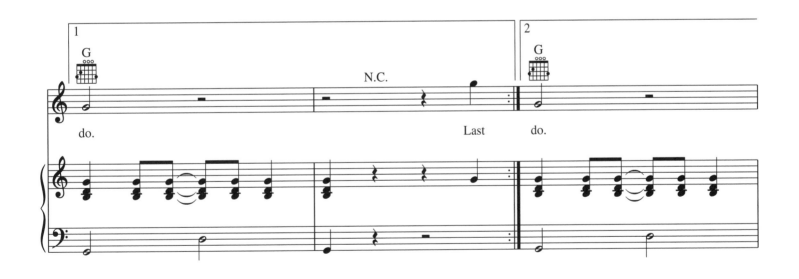

1
do.

2
Last do.

I've noth-in' to do.

Repeat and Fade

Optional Ending

FOGGY MOUNTAIN BREAKDOWN

Words and Music by
EARL SCRUGGS

FOLSOM PRISON BLUES

Words and Music by
JOHN R. CASH

Moderately (not too slow)

Chorus

1. I

hear the train a - com - in'; it's roll - in' 'round the bend, And

I was just a ba - by my ma - ma told me son, _____

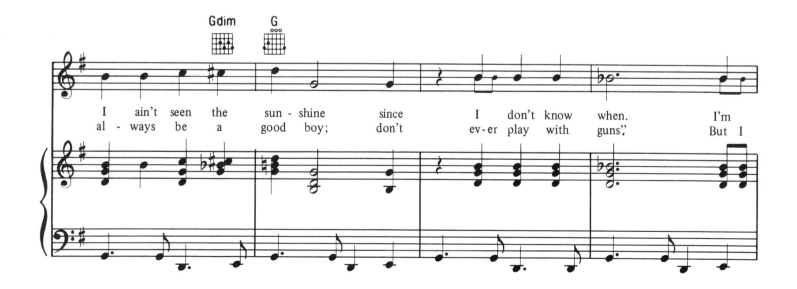

I ain't seen the sun - shine since I don't know when. I'm

al - ways be a good boy; don't ev - er play with guns," But I

stuck at Fol - som Pris - on and time keeps drag - gin' on. ___
shot a man in Re - no just ___ to watch him die. ___

But that train keeps roll - in'
When I hear that whis - tle blow - in'

1,2,3, 4

on down to San ___ An - tone. ___ When ___
I hang my head ___ and ___ cry. ___

3. I bet there's rich folks eatin' in a fancy dining car.
   They're prob'ly drinkin' coffee and smokin' big cigars,
   But I know I had it comin', I know I can't be free,
   But those people keep a-movin', and that's what tortures me.

4. Well, if they freed me from this prison, if that railroad train was mine,
   I bet I'd move on over a little farther down the line,
   Far from Folsom Prison, that's where I want to stay,
   And I'd let that lonesome whistle blow my blues away.

FOREVER AND EVER, AMEN

Words and Music by PAUL OVERSTREET
and DON SCHLITZ

THE GAMBLER

Words and Music by
DON SCHLITZ

164

166

FRIENDS IN LOW PLACES

Words and Music by DEWAYNE BLACKWELL
and EARL BUD LEE

170

Well, I

I've got friends __ in low plac - es where the

whis - key _____ drowns _____ and the beer _____ chas - es my blues _____

GALVESTON

Words and Music by
JIM WEBB

Moderately

Gal - ves - ton, ____ oh, Gal - ves -
Gal - ves - ton, ____ oh, Gal - ves -

ton,
ton,
I still hear ____ your sea - winds ___
I still hear ____ your sea - waves ___

blow - ing; ___
crash - in', ___
I still see ____ her dark eyes
while I watch ____ the can - nons

GO REST HIGH ON THAT MOUNTAIN

Words and Music by
VINCE GILL

Slowly, in Gospel style

1. I know your

life   on __ earth was trou-bled __ and on - ly you _____ could know __ the
2. *(See additional lyrics)*

Additional Lyrics

2. Oh, how we cried the day you left us,
   We gathered 'round your grave to grieve.
   I wish I could see the angels' faces
   When they hear your sweet voice sing.
   Chorus

GOD BLESS THE U.S.A.

Words and Music by
LEE GREENWOOD

A GOOD HEARTED WOMAN

Words and Music by WILLIE NELSON
and WAYLON JENNINGS

188

GREEN GREEN GRASS OF HOME

Words and Music by
CURLY PUTMAN

191

GUITARS, CADILLACS

Words and Music by
DWIGHT YOAKAM

194

There ain't no glam -

HARPER VALLEY P.T.A.

Words and Music by
TOM T. HALL

Moderately (with a heavy beat)

I want to tell you all a stor-y 'bout a Har-per Val-ley wid-owed wife_____
note said, "Mis-ses John-son, you're wear-ing your dres-ses way too high;
hap-pened that the P. T. A. was gon-na meet that ver-y af-ter-noon;

Who had a teen-age daugh-ter who at-tend-ed, Har-per Val-ley Jun-ior
It's re-port-ed you've been drink-ing and a-run-nin' 'round with men and go-ing
They were sure sur-prised when Mis-ses John-son wore her mi-ni-skirt in-to the

high.
wild:
room.

Well her daugh-ter came home__ one af-ter
And we don't be-lieve you ought to be a-
And as she walked up to the black-board, I

200

HAVE I TOLD YOU LATELY THAT I LOVE YOU

Words and Music by
SCOTT WISEMAN

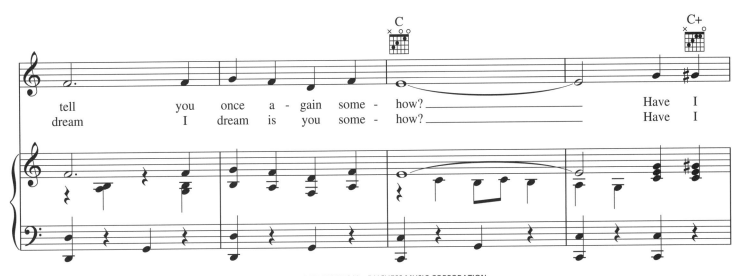

HE STOPPED LOVING HER TODAY

Words and Music by BOBBY BRADDOCK
and CURLY PUTMAN

Verse 3:
He kept some letters by his bed, dated 1962.
He had underlined in red every single, "I love you".

Verse 4:
I went to see him just today, oh, but I didn't see no tears;
All dressed up to go away, first time I'd seen him smile in years.
(To Chorus:)

Verse 5: *(Spoken)*
You know, she came to see him one last time.
We all wondered if she would.
And it came running through my mind,
This time he's over her for good. (To Chorus:)

HE'LL HAVE TO GO

Words and Music by JOE ALLISON
and AUDREY ALLISON

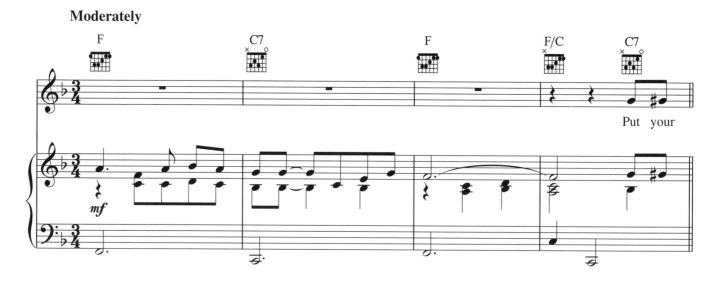

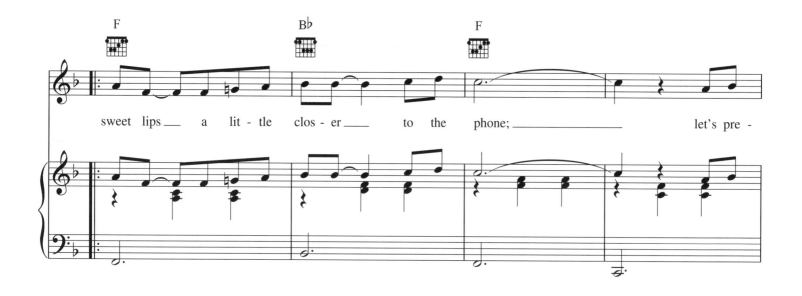

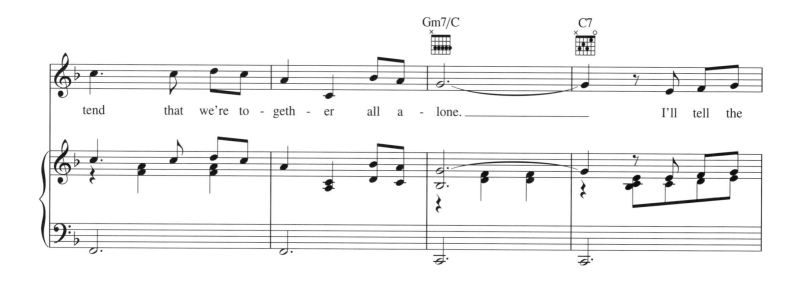

208

HELLO DARLIN'

Words and Music by
CONWAY TWITTY

HELLO WALLS

Words and Music by
WILLIE NELSON

ceil-ing,_____ I'm gon-na stare at you a-while you know I

can't sleep, so won't you bear with me a-while? We must

all pull to-geth-er or else I'll lose my mind, 'cause I've got a

feel-in' she'll be gone a long, long time._____

HERE'S A QUARTER
(Call Someone Who Cares)

Words and Music by
TRAVIS TRITT

HEY, GOOD LOOKIN'

Words and Music by
HANK WILLIAMS

Moderately

I AM A MAN OF CONSTANT SORROW

Words and Music by
CARTER STANLEY

sor - row. _____ I've seen trou - ble all ___ my
trou - ble, _____ no pleas - ure here _____ on earth ___ I've
lov - er, _____ I nev - er ex - pect _____ to see ___ you a -
val - ley _____ for man - y years _____ where I ___ may lay,
stran - ger; _____ my face ___ you nev - er will see ___ no

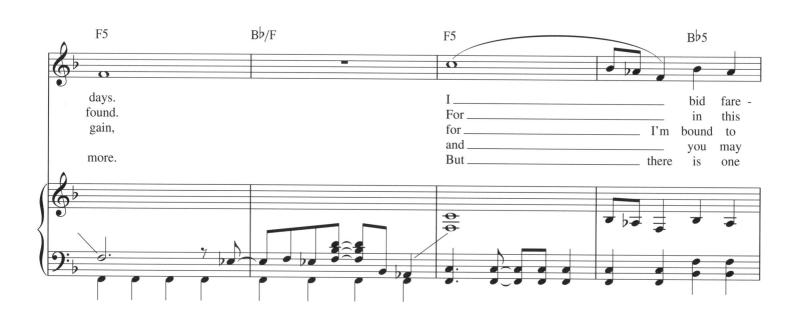

days. I _____ bid fare -
found. For _____ in this
gain, for _____ I'm bound to
more. and _____ you may
But _____ there is one

well _____ to old ___ Ken - tuck - y, _____ the place _ where I _____
world _____ I'm bound _ to ram - ble; _____ I have _ no friends
ride _____ that North - ern rail - road; _____ per - haps _ I'll die _____
learn _____ to love _ an - oth - er _____ while I ___ am sleep -
prom - ise that is giv - en: _____ I'll meet _ you on _____

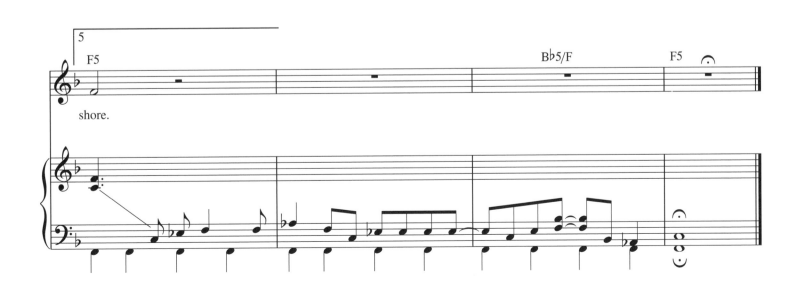

I CAN'T STOP LOVING YOU

Words and Music by
DON GIBSON

I'D BE BETTER OFF
(In a Pine Box)

Words and Music by JOHNNY MacRAE
and STEVE CLARK

proved _____ that I _____ was wrong. _____ And
spread _____ your wings _____ and fly. _____ But,

when your _____ eyes _____ met _____ mine _____ I knew _____ that
when I _____ saw _____ the lov - in' way _____ you

you _ were gone _ for - ev - er _____
held _____ on _ to each oth - er _____

a -
it was

I FALL TO PIECES

Words and Music by HANK COCHRAN
and HARLAN HOWARD

Moderate Country 2

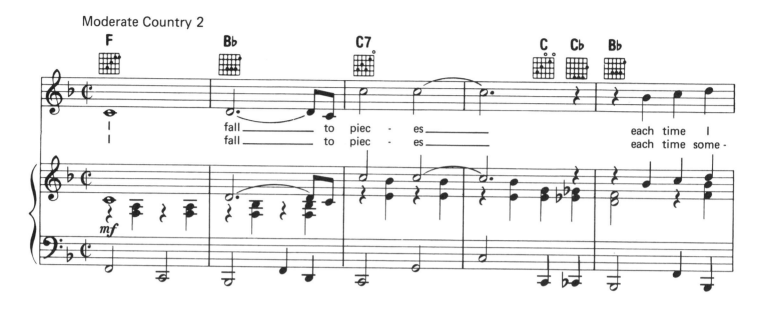

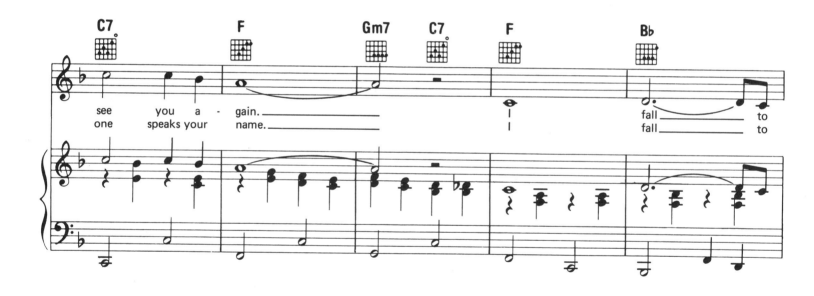

I HOPE YOU DANCE

Words and Music by TIA SILLERS
and MARK D. SANDERS

I WALK THE LINE

Words and Music by
JOHN R. CASH

3. As sure as night is dark and day is light,
   I keep you on my mind both day and night.
   And happiness I've known proves that it's right.
   Because you're mine I Walk The Line.

4. You've got a way to keep me on your side.
   You give me cause for love that I can't hide.
   For you I know I'd even try to turn the tide.
   Because you're mine I Walk The Line.

5. I keep a close watch on this heart of mine.
   I keep my eyes wide open all the time.
   I keep the ends out for the tie that binds.
   Because you're mine I Walk The Line.

I WILL ALWAYS LOVE YOU

Words and Music by
DOLLY PARTON

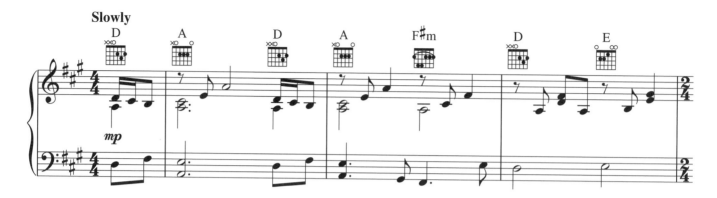

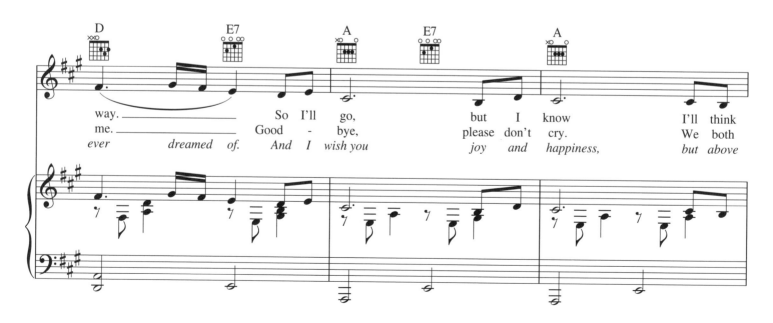

I'M SO LONESOME I COULD CRY

Words and Music by
HANK WILLIAMS

IF YOU'VE GOT THE MONEY
(I've Got the Time)

Words and Music by LEFTY FRIZZELL
and JIM BECK

Moderately (in 2)

If you've got the mon - ey, I've got the time,____

We'll go honk - y tonk - in' and we'll have a time. We'll make all the
Bring a - long your

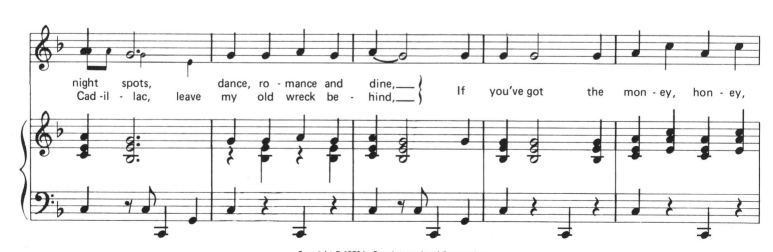

night spots, dance, ro - mance and dine,____ } If you've got
Cad - il - lac, leave my old wreck be - hind,____ the mon - ey, hon - ey,

INDEPENDENCE DAY

Words and Music by
GRETCHEN PETERS

Well, she seemed _

all right _ by dawn's _ ear-ly light, _ though she
gets a-round in a small, small town; _ they
up the sky that fourth _ of Ju - ly, _ by the

looked a lit-tle wor-ried and weak. _ She
said he was a dan-ger-ous man. _ But
time that the fire-men come. _ They just

258

IT WASN'T GOD WHO MADE HONKY TONK ANGELS

Words and Music by
J.D. MILLER

IS THERE LIFE OUT THERE

Words and Music by RICK GILES
and SUSAN LONGACRE

IT'S YOUR LOVE

Words and Music by
STEPHONY E. SMITH

KILLIN' TIME

Words and Music by CLINT BLACK
and HAYDEN NICHOLAS

KING OF THE ROAD

Words and Music by
ROGER MILLER

(1., D.S.) Trail - er ___ for sale ___ or rent, ___ rooms ___ to let, fif - ty cents. ___
(2.) Third box - car mid - night train, ___ des - ti - na - tion: Ban - gor, Maine. ___

No phone, _ no pool, _ no pets; ___ I ain't got no cig - a - rettes. _ Ah, but
Old worn - out suit _ and shoes; ___ I don't pay no un - ion dues. _ I smoke

two hours ___ of push - ing broom ___ buys a eight ___ by twelve four bit room. ___ } I'm a
old sto - gies I have found, _ short ___ but not too big a - round. ___

KISS AN ANGEL GOOD MORNIN'

Words and Music by
BEN PETERS

LOVESICK BLUES

Words by IRVING MILLS
Music by CLIFF FRIEND

MAKE THE WORLD GO AWAY

Words and Music by
HANK COCHRAN

MAMA HE'S CRAZY

Words and Music by
KENNY O'DELL

Moderately slow, but flowing

Ma-ma,___ I found some~one,___ like you said would come a-long.
Ma-ma,___ you al-ways said,___ bet-ter look be-fore you leap.

He's a sight,___ so un-like___ an-y man I've known. I
May-be so,___ but here I go___ let my heart___ lead me. He

was a-fraid to let him in 'cause I'm not the trust-in' kind, but
thinks I hung the moon and stars, I think he's a liv-in' dream, well

OKIE FROM MUSKOGEE

Words and Music by MERLE HAGGARD
and ROY EDWARD BURRIS

1. We don't smoke mar - i - jua - na in Mus - ko - gee,
2. We don't make a par - ty out of lov - ing,
boots are still in style if a man needs foot - wear,

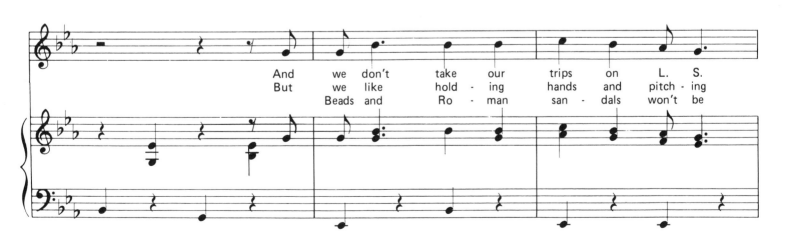

And we don't take our trips on L. S.
But we like hold - ing hands and pitch - ing
Beads and Ro - man san - dals won't be

MAMMAS DON'T LET YOUR BABIES GROW UP TO BE COWBOYS

Words and Music by ED BRUCE
and PATSY BRUCE

Country Waltz

Mam - mas don't let your ba - bies grow up __ to be cow - boys.

Don't let 'em pick gui - tars and

drive them old trucks. Make 'em be doc - tors and law - yers and

MY HOME'S IN ALABAMA

Words and Music by TEDDY GENTRY
and RANDY OWEN

ON THE OTHER HAND

Words and Music by DON SCHLITZ
and PAUL OVERSTREET

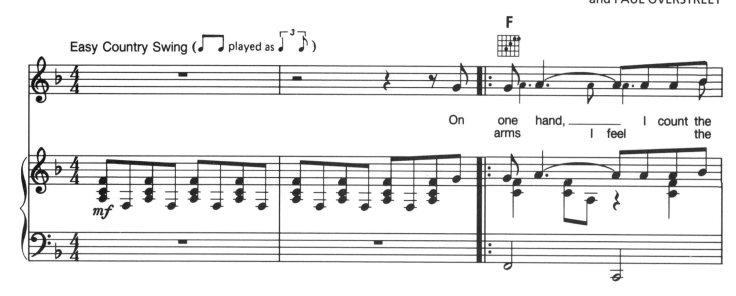

On one hand, _____ I feel I count the
arms _____ I feel the

rea-sons _____ I could stay with you, _____ and hold you close to
pas-sion _____ I thought had died. _____ When I looked in-to your

me all night long I found my-self. _____ So man-y _____ lov-ers'
eyes _____ When I first _____ kissed your

On one hand I could stay and be your lov-ing man,

but the rea - son I must go is on the oth-er hand.

In your Yeah, the

rea - son I must go is on the oth-er hand.

8va bassa

RHINESTONE COWBOY

Words and Music by
LARRY WEISS

PASSIONATE KISSES

Words and Music by
LUCINDA WILLIAMS

Is___ it too much to ask?___ I want a com-fort-a-ble bed___ that won't
Is___ it too much to de-mand?___ I want a full house___ and a

PLEASE REMEMBER ME

Words and Music by RODNEY CROWELL
and WILL JENNINGS

Original key: D♭ major. This edition has been transposed down one half-step to be more playable.

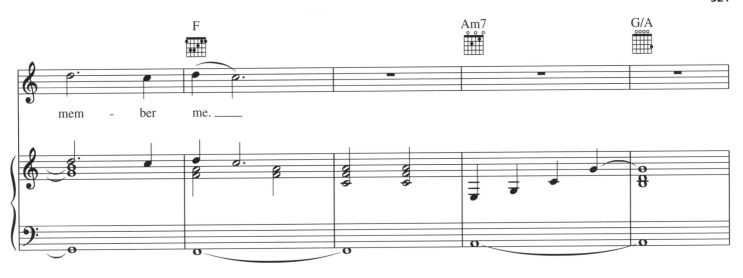

mem - ber me. ____

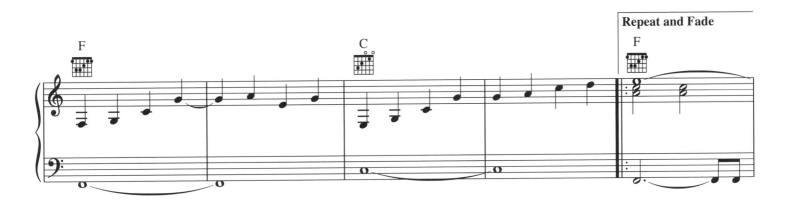

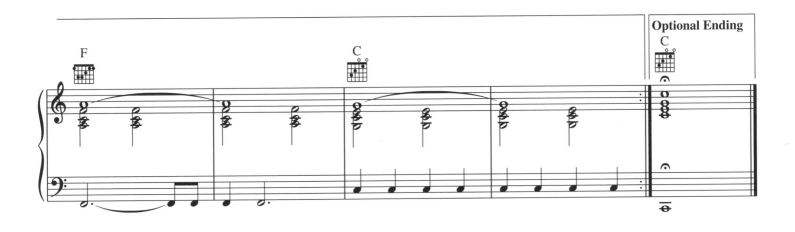

RING OF FIRE

Words and Music by MERLE KILGORE
and JUNE CARTER

Moderately bright

Love _____ is a burn - ing
taste _____ of love is

thing, _____ and it
sweet, _____ when

(I Never Promised You A)
ROSE GARDEN

Words and Music by
JOE SOUTH

Moderately Bright, with a beat

I beg your par - don, I nev - er prom - ised you a rose ___ gar - den.

A - long with the sun - shine, there's got to be a lit - tle rain_ some - time.

When you take you got to give, so live and let live ___ or let

330

SEVEN YEAR ACHE

Words and Music by
ROSANNE CASH

SHE'S IN LOVE WITH THE BOY

Words and Music by
JON IMS

*Recorded a half step lower.

She'd fol - low Tom - my an - y - where.—
Kat - ie looks at Tom - my like I still look at you." } She's in

love with the boy. She's in love with the boy. She's in

love with the boy.

{ 1.2. And e - ven if they have to run a -
{ 3. What's meant to be will al - ways find a

To Coda

SHOULD'VE BEEN A COWBOY

Words and Music by
TOBY KEITH

Additional Lyrics

2. I might have had a side-kick with a funny name
Runnin' wild through the hills chasin' Jesse James
Or endin' up on the brink of danger
Ridin' shot-gun for the Texas Rangers
Go west young man, haven't you been told
California's full of whiskey, women, and gold
Sleepin' out all night, beneath the desert stars
With a dream in my eye and a prayer in my heart
To Chorus:

SMOKY MOUNTAIN RAIN

Words and Music by KYE FLEMING
and DENNIS MORGAN

SOMETHING IN RED

Words and Music by
ANGELA KASET

Moderately, with a lilt

I'm look - ing for __ some - thing in
look - ing for __ some - thing in

red.
green.

Some - thing that's __ shock - ing, to turn __ some - one's __
Some - thing to __ out - do an ex - high school __

head.
queen.

Strap - less and __ se - quined and cut __ down to there, __
Jeal - ous - y __ comes in the col - or of jade. __

STAND BY YOUR MAN

Words and Music by TAMMY WYNETTE
and BILLY SHERRILL

STRAWBERRY WINE

Words and Music by MATRACA BERG
and GARY HARRISON

Original key: Db major. This edition has been transposed up one half-step to be more playable.

SUNDAY MORNIN' COMIN' DOWN

Words and Music by
KRIS KRISTOFFERSON

SWEET DREAMS

Words and Music by
DON GIBSON

369

TAKE ME HOME, COUNTRY ROADS

Words and Music by JOHN DENVER,
BILL DANOFF and TAFFY NIVERT

TAKE THIS JOB AND SHOVE IT

Words and Music by
DAVID ALLEN COE

I've seen a lot of good folk die that had a lot of bills to pay.
One of these days I'm gon-na blow my top. That suck-er, he's gon-na pay.

I'd give the shirt right off of my back if I had the guts to say:
Lord, I can't wait to see their fac-es when I get the nerve to say:

more. Take this job and

shove it!

TENNESSEE WALTZ

Words and Music by REDD STEWART
and PEE WEE KING

THERE STANDS THE GLASS

Words by RUSS HULL, MARY JEAN SHURTZ
and AUDREY GREISHAM
Music by RUSS HULL

WALKING THE FLOOR OVER YOU

Words and Music by
ERNEST TUBB

Swingy tempo

Eb   C7   F7

1. You left me and you went a way
2. (Now,) Dar - ling, you know I love you well
3. (Now,) some - day you may be lone - some too

Bb7   Eb

You said that you'd be back in just a day
Love you more than I can ev - er tell
Walk - ing the floor is good for you

WHEN I CALL YOUR NAME

Words and Music by VINCE GILL
and TIM DUBOIS

WHEN YOU SAY NOTHING AT ALL

Words and Music by PAUL OVERSTREET
and DON SCHLITZ

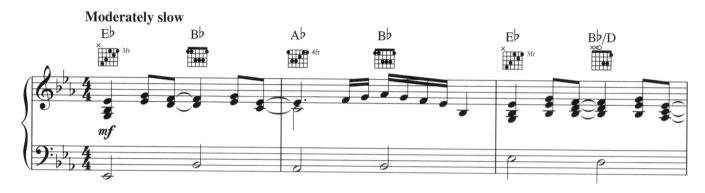

It's a-maz - ing how _ you can speak right _ to my heart. _
All day long _ I can hear peo - ple talk - ing out loud, _

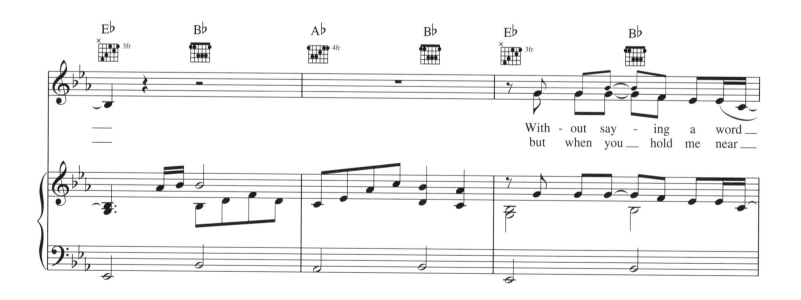

With - out say - ing a word _
but when you _ hold me near _

when you say noth-ing at all. _____

The

when you say noth-ing at all. _____

WHERE WERE YOU
(When the World Stopped Turning)

Words and Music by
ALAN JACKSON

WIDE OPEN SPACES

Words and Music by
SUSAN GIBSON

Who does-n't know what I'm talk-ing a-bout?___

As her folks drive a - way, her dad yells, "Check the oil."

Mom stares out the win - dow and says, "I'm leav - in' my girl." She said, "It

YOU ARE MY SUNSHINE

Words and Music by JIMMIE DAVIS
and CHARLES MITCHELL

YOU'RE STILL THE ONE

Words and Music by SHANIA TWAIN
and R.J. LANGE

412

YOUR CHEATIN' HEART

Words and Music by
HANK WILLIAMS